Let's FLY!

BARRINGTON IRVING'S RECORD-BREAKING FLIGHT AROUND THE WORLD

written by **Barrington Irving** and **Chana Stiefel**
illustrated by **Shamar Knight-Justice**

DIAL BOOKS FOR YOUNG READERS

To the greatest love of my life,
my wife, Dianella, and my reason and
motivation, my children, Chilly, Skyler,
Madison, and Naomi —B.I.

To my children and their big
adventures ahead! —C.S.

For Caiden—may you always see
the sky and reach for it. —S.K.-J.

Dial Books for Young Readers ⬤ An imprint of Penguin Random House LLC, New York
First published in the United States of America by Dial Books for Young Readers,
an imprint of Penguin Random House LLC, 2024
Text copyright © 2024 by Chana Stiefel and Barrington Irving
Illustrations copyright © 2024 by Shamar Knight-Justice
Photographs courtesy of Barrington Irving
Visit us online at PenguinRandomHouse.com.
Library of Congress Cataloging-in-Publication Data is available. • ISBN 9780593532133
10 9 8 7 6 5 4 3 2 1
Manufactured in India • THO
Design by Sylvia Bi • Text set in Mohr • This art was created digitally with mixed media elements in Procreate.
This is a work of nonfiction. Some names and identifying details have been changed.

I'm a dream chaser. A solo flier. A world-record breaker. I'm Barrington Irving.
People said I'd never make my dreams come true. But I powered through!
Want to know how? Buckle up!

Flight controls . . . check. Fuel . . . check. Electrical power on.
Cockpit door locked. Start the engine.
Ground control, ready for takeoff—

LET'S FLY!

wHOOSH!

That jewel of an island is Jamaica—where I was born.

CLANK!

I helped my uncle fix cars.

Then I built my own.

ZOOM!

ZOOM!

Blue skies over Miami, where we moved when I was six.
Coconut palms pushed through hot concrete . . . anything was possible!

From the sky, everything seems small, even problems.

Like when school didn't feel safe.

"Why do you talk funny?"

"Where'd you get those clothes?"
"What kind of sneakers are those?"

I shrank inside, but all that badgering pumped me with fuel.
I promised myself, "I'm going to SOAR!"

In high school, playing football seemed like my ticket to success.

Then, out of the blue, Captain Gary Robinson—a man I'd never met before—swooped into my life. He walked into my parents' Miami bookstore one day and asked me a single question that changed my destiny: "Have you ever thought of becoming a pilot?"

I'd never seen a Black pilot before!
"Don't you need to be a genius?" I asked.
Captain Robinson smiled. "You need to have a passion for what you do."

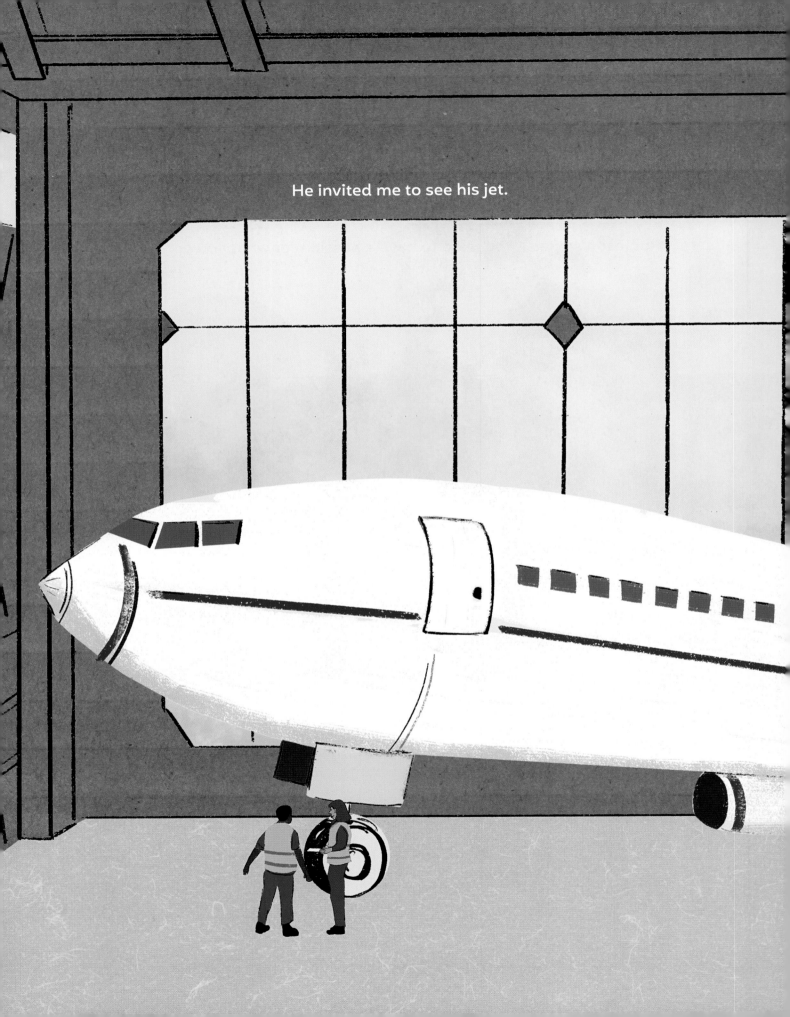

He invited me to see his jet.

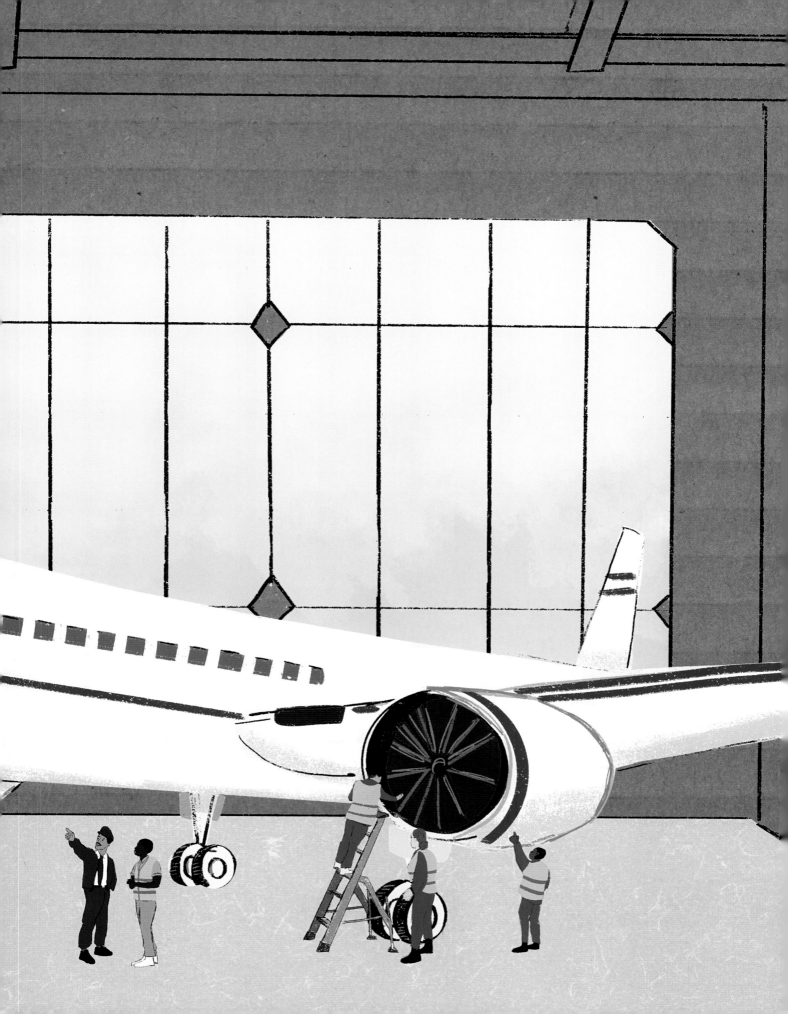

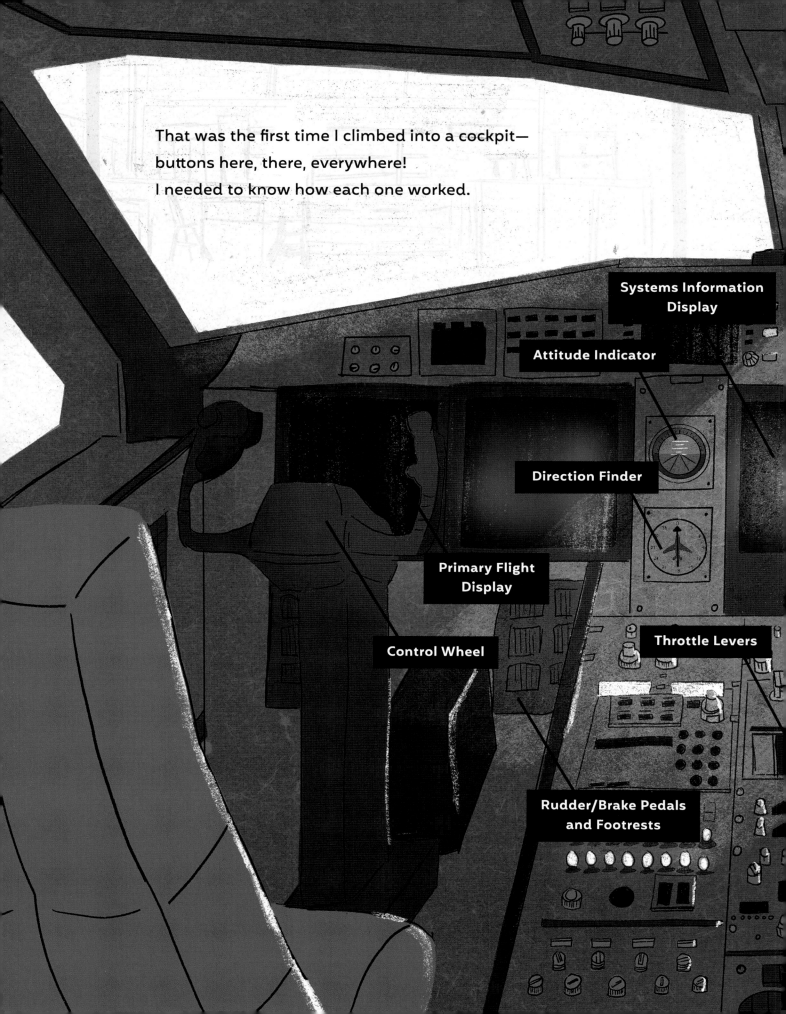

That was the first time I climbed into a cockpit—
buttons here, there, everywhere!
I needed to know how each one worked.

Systems Information
Display

Attitude Indicator

Direction Finder

Primary Flight
Display

Control Wheel

Throttle Levers

Rudder/Brake Pedals
and Footrests

For my sixteenth birthday,
Captain Robinson gave me the best gift—
my first flight with an instructor!

WHOAAA!

That bumpy air tied my stomach in knots.
But when the city shrinks beneath your wings, you
become a soaring bird. You just want to fly–fly–fly!

But how?

Not so fast.

When I was twenty-one, Captain Robinson threw me a challenge.

"I helped you," he reminded me. "Now you help someone else."

"Roger that, Captain!"

I started an after-school program to share my passion for flying.

But I still wanted to do something HUGE to inspire kids to reach for the sky.

Maybe I'll fly around Florida.

Not big enough.

Fly cross-country?

Not exciting enough.

That's when my BIG IDEA struck. I'd fly around the WORLD—by myself.
There was just one small problem. I needed wings!

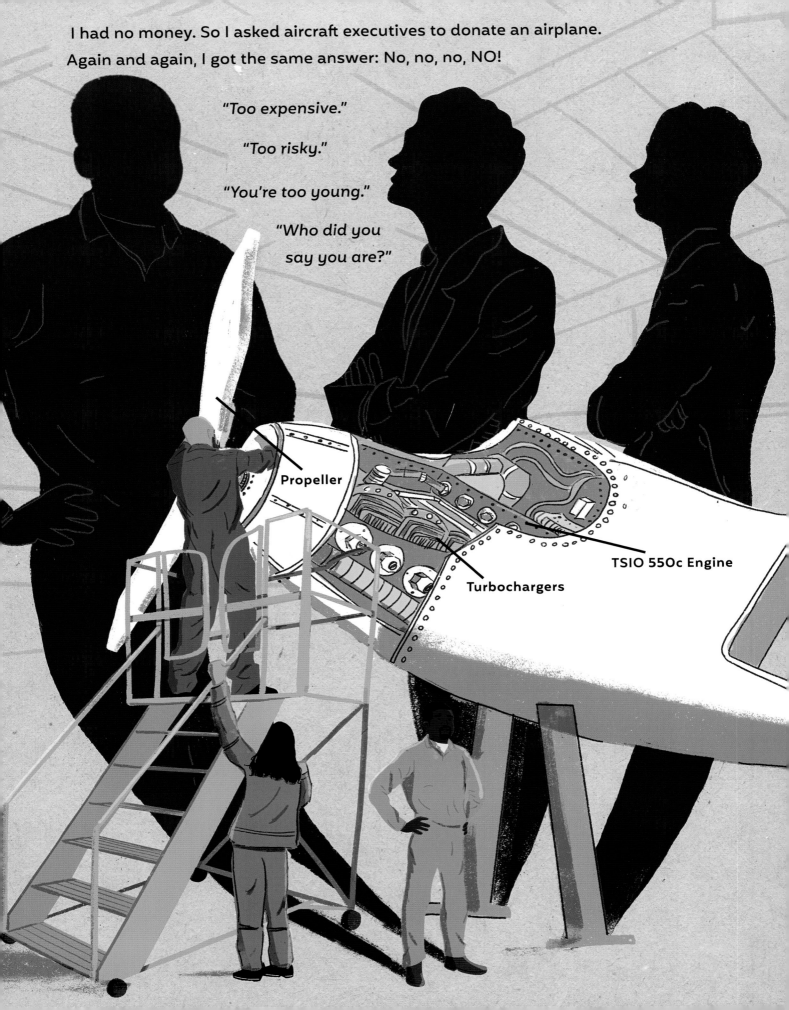

If one company wouldn't give me a whole airplane,
maybe several companies would donate the parts.

For two years, I shared my round-the-world dream . . .

"Can you . . .?"
"Would you please . . .?"
"Any chance . . .?"

Until one manufacturer offered me an engine.
Soon other companies donated more parts.
A team of engineers helped me build it.

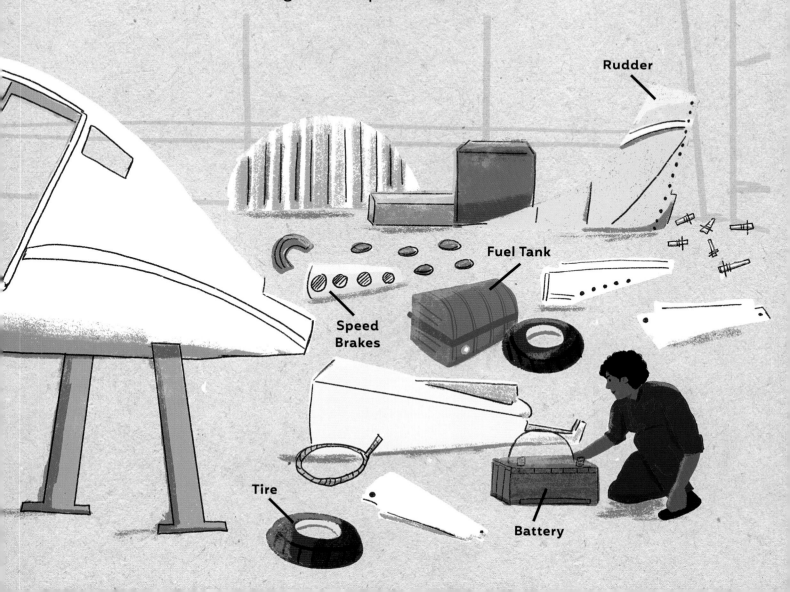

Rudder

Fuel Tank

Speed
Brakes

Tire

Battery

I called it . . .

ration

For a full year, I planned my route.

Where should I stop? How could I train? What should I pack?

At last! The Big Day.

My worries swirled like a tornado when I climbed into the cockpit.

My plane has no weather radar. What about storms?

What if I crash into the ocean? I can't swim!

I'm just twenty-three years old.

Am I ready to fly around
the world by myself?

Too late to turn back.
A sea of schoolchildren
were waving and cheering!

I could NOT let them down.

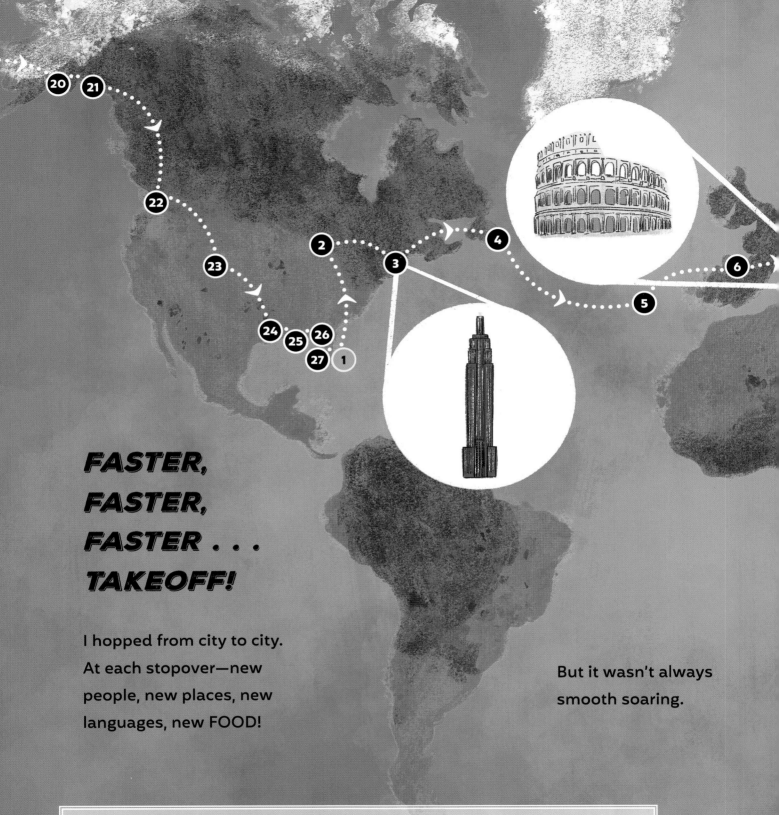

FASTER, FASTER, FASTER . . . TAKEOFF!

I hopped from city to city. At each stopover—new people, new places, new languages, new FOOD!

But it wasn't always smooth soaring.

BARRINGTON'S COMPLETE FLIGHT PATH

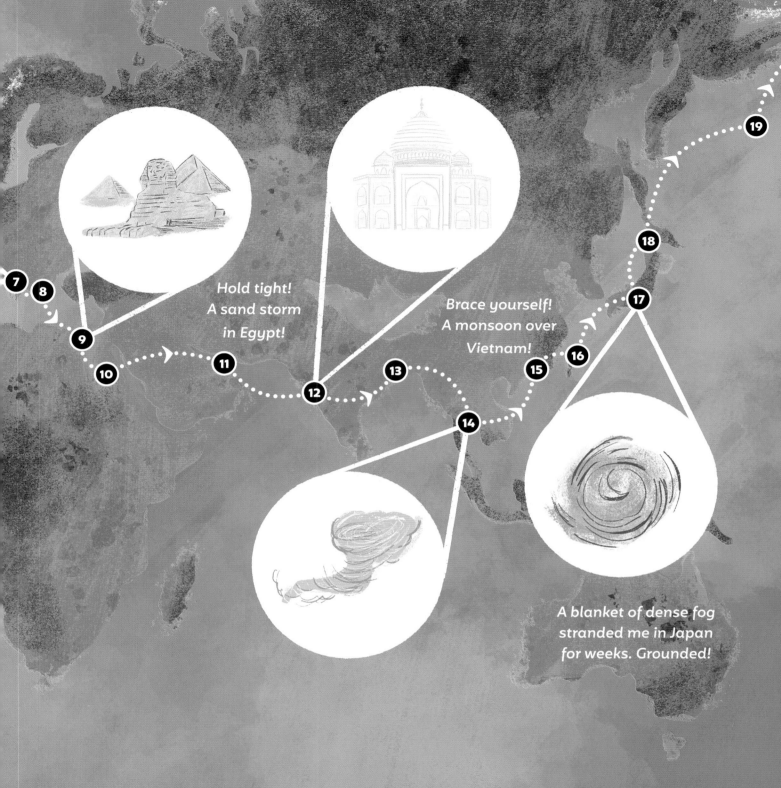

Hold tight!
A sand storm
in Egypt!

Brace yourself!
A monsoon over
Vietnam!

A blanket of dense fog
stranded me in Japan
for weeks. Grounded!

My heart ached for my family. I missed my mom's cooking. I dreaded crossing the frigid North Pacific. Ten hours flying over choppy seas. Should I give up? People around the world were waiting for me.

Finally, a break in the fog. Airborne once again!

Over the Pacific, wicked gusts shook my plane like a saltshaker.
Violent storms threatened my route. I risked climbing above the clouds.
Higher and higher!

I shivered in my flight suit.
Low pressure wore me out.

My fingers turned blue.
I breathed bottled oxygen.
Ice formed on the wings.

HANG ON!

I logged 26,800 miles in 97 days with 26 stops in 12 countries.

Touching down in Miami, I made history.
I became the youngest person
and first Black man to fly
solo around the world.

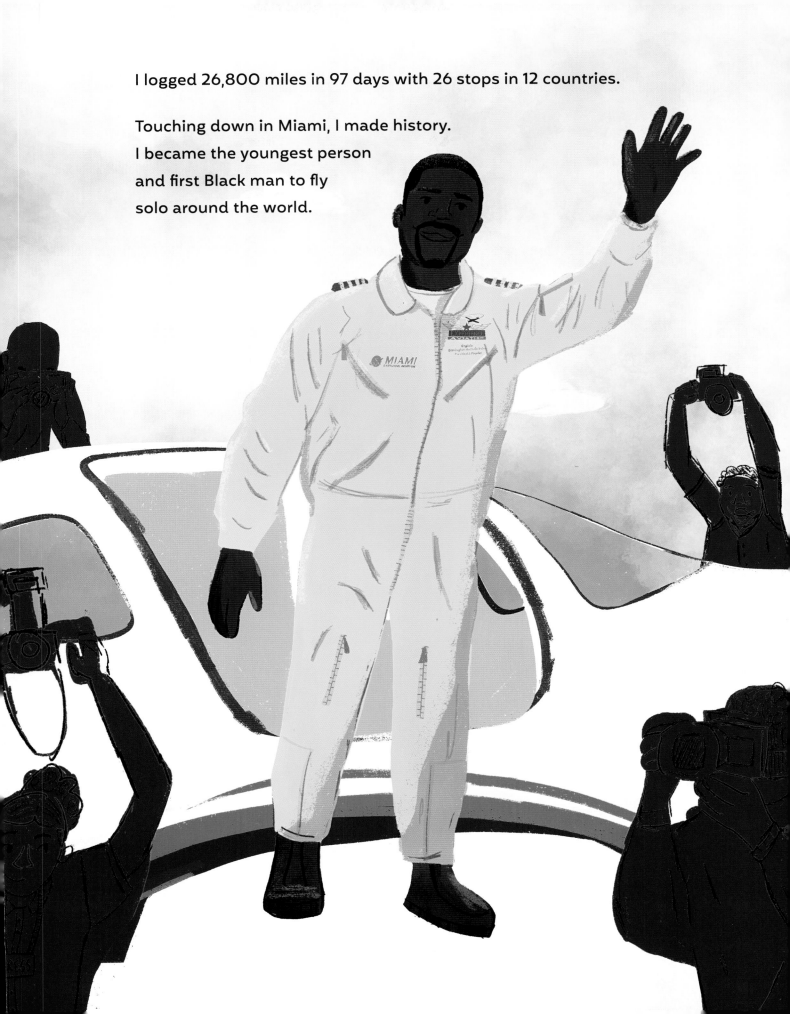

I hugged my family and Captain Robinson.
But the adventure doesn't end there . . .

Because here you are,
soaring with me.

So what's your dream?

LET'S FLY!

SOME RECORDS ARE MEANT TO BE BROKEN

Barrington will always hold the record as the first Black man to fly solo around the world. On his journey, he also broke 11 speed records for a single-engine aircraft traveling from one place to another.

In 2012, Carlo Schmid, a twenty two-year-old Swiss pilot, broke Barrington's record as the youngest pilot to fly solo around the world. Then in 2014, Schmid's record was broken by nineteen-year-old American pilot Matt Guthmiller. The record was broken again in 2016, 2018, and 2021. Currently, the record is held by Mack Rutherford, a British-Belgian pilot, who took off at the age of sixteen and turned seventeen in flight to become the youngest person ever to fly solo around the world, landing on August 24, 2022. On January 20, 2022, his sister Zara Rutherford, at age nineteen, became the youngest female pilot to do so. She broke the previous record held by Shaesta Waiz, an Afghan-American pilot who was mentored by Barrington and broke the record at age thirty in 2017. Who'll be next? Maybe YOU!

FAB FACTS

✈ Barrington left Miami with only thirty dollars in his pocket—not even enough money to fill his fuel tank. But by the time he landed at his first stop in Cleveland, Ohio, he had raised $100,000 in sponsorships—the money provided by businesses and individuals to support events like Barrington's around-the-world flight.

✈ In total, the trip raised $1.3 million in sponsorships to cover the costs.

✈ Barrington lost thirty pounds in three months of flying around the world. It was tough to eat meals while flying for long stretches of time. Instead he relied on snack bars, bananas, and energy drinks.

✈ *Inspiration* didn't have a bathroom on board. Barrington used a pee tube, but that was difficult to do while wearing a bulky flight suit. Sometimes he just had to hold it in!

✈ Even before he took flight on *Inspiration*, Barrington founded Experience Aviation, an after-school program to teach kids about aviation and STEM (Science, Technology, Engineering, and Math). As of now, more than 5,000 students have completed the program. Many have gone into STEM careers as pilots, aircrafts mechanics, air traffic controllers, flight instructors, line service technicians (who service private jets), aerospace engineers, and more. Learn more at experienceaviation.org.

✈ Shortly after his historic flight around the world, Barrington challenged a group of Experience Aviation kids to build an aircraft in just ten weeks. He told them, "If you build it, I'll fly it!" They did—and so did he!

✈ In 2014, Barrington turned a jet into a Flying Classroom. Kids across the country—from kindergarten through eighth grade—can join him virtually on scientific adventures all over the world. He's led more than sixty-seven STEM expeditions on six continents, exploring bat caves in the Bahamas, learning about tiny microbes living in an Alaskan glacier, studying lava flow in Hawaii, investigating layers of the Amazon rainforest, and more. Find out more at flyingclassroom.com.

TIME FLIES!

1983 (November 11)
Barrington Irving is born in Kingston, Jamaica.

1989
The Irving family moves to Miami.

1999
Barrington meets Captain Robinson at his parents' bookstore.

2002
Barrington graduates high school. He turns down football scholarships to go to flight school.

2002
Barrington wins a full scholarship from FMU and the U.S. Air Force to cover college tuition and flight training.

2002
At the age of nineteen, Barrington earns his first pilot's license to fly small planes. He decides he wants to study aeronautics and become a commercial pilot.

2005
Barrington starts Experience Aviation, a non-profit educational program to teach kids about careers in aviation.

2005
Barrington drives twelve hours from Miami to Mobile, Alabama, for an unscheduled meeting with the president of Continental Motors. A few weeks later, the president calls Barrington. He donates an $83,000 airplane engine. Afterward, many other companies donate parts too.

2007
(March 23) Barrington takes off from Miami for his round-the-world trip. (June 27) Barrington returns, becoming the youngest person and first Black pilot to fly solo around the world.

2008
Barrington takes off in *Inspiration 2*, a plane built by sixty Miami high school students as part of Experience Aviation's "Build and Soar" summer program.

2009
Barrington graduates FMU.

2014
Barrington turns a jet into a Flying Classroom.

"YEAH, I SAID THAT." QUOTES FROM BARRINGTON IRVING:

"The only person who can stop you from doing something great is you."

"The secret is having the dream in the first place."

"I like to do things people say I can't."

"Just take the first step. Whether you trip or stumble, you're still moving forward."

BIBLIOGRAPHY

Irving, Barrington, and Holly Peppe. *Touch the Sky: My Solo Flight Around the World.* New York: Scholastic, 2012.

Peppe, Holly. *Dream, Live Fly: A World Flight Adventure, The Barrington Irving Story.*
[unpublished manuscript that became *Touch the Sky*]

Stiefel, Chana with Peppe, Holly. *Sky High: Two Men Who Couldn't Keep Their Feet on the Ground.* New York: Scholastic, 2012.

"Barrington Irving: Teaching from the Skies," National Geographic Live, August 27, 2012.
https://youtu.be/DmknAhSdjME

"Barrington Irving: Got 30 Dollars in My Pocket," NOVA. July 3, 2014,
https://youtu.be/JJAd8HoFNKM

"Barrington Irving: From the Island to the Sky," TEDXJamaica, November 2, 2011.
https://youtu.be/4yrvZZGnxHA

"Barrington Irving: Explorer Since 2012," *National Geographic.*
https://www.nationalgeographic.org/find-explorers/barrington-irving

Malozzi, Vincent M. "At 23, the Youngest Pilot to Solo the Planet." *The New York Times,* July 18, 2007.
https://www.nytimes.com/2007/07/18/nyregion/18pilot.html

Samson, Alyssa. "Pilot and Educator: Barrington Irving." *National Geographic,* updated February 8, 2024.
https://education.nationalgeographic.org/resource/real-world-geography-barrington-irving/

Experience Aviation: https://www.experienceaviation.org/

Flying Classroom: https://flyingclassroom.com/

Martin, Michelle, "African Americans Fly High with Math and Science," NPR, Tell Me More, February, 4, 2013.
https://www.npr.org/2013/02/04/171065162/african-americans-fly-high-with-math-and-science

Phone interviews with author Chana Stiefel and Barrington Irving,
July 21, 2010, October 19, 2016, December 28, 2016.
In-person meeting January 24, 2017.